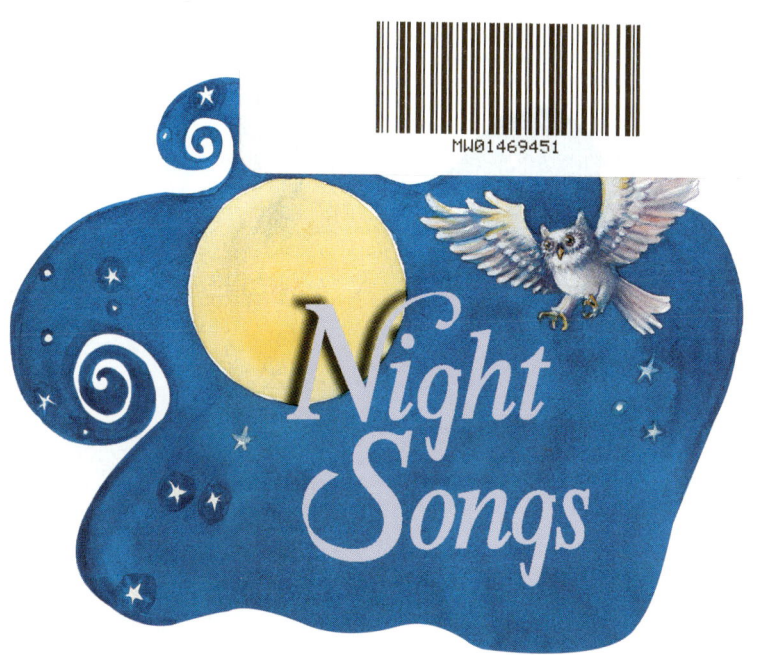

Night Songs

by Linda Yoshizawa
illustrated by Kathleen McCord

MODERN CURRICULUM PRESS
Pearson Learning Group

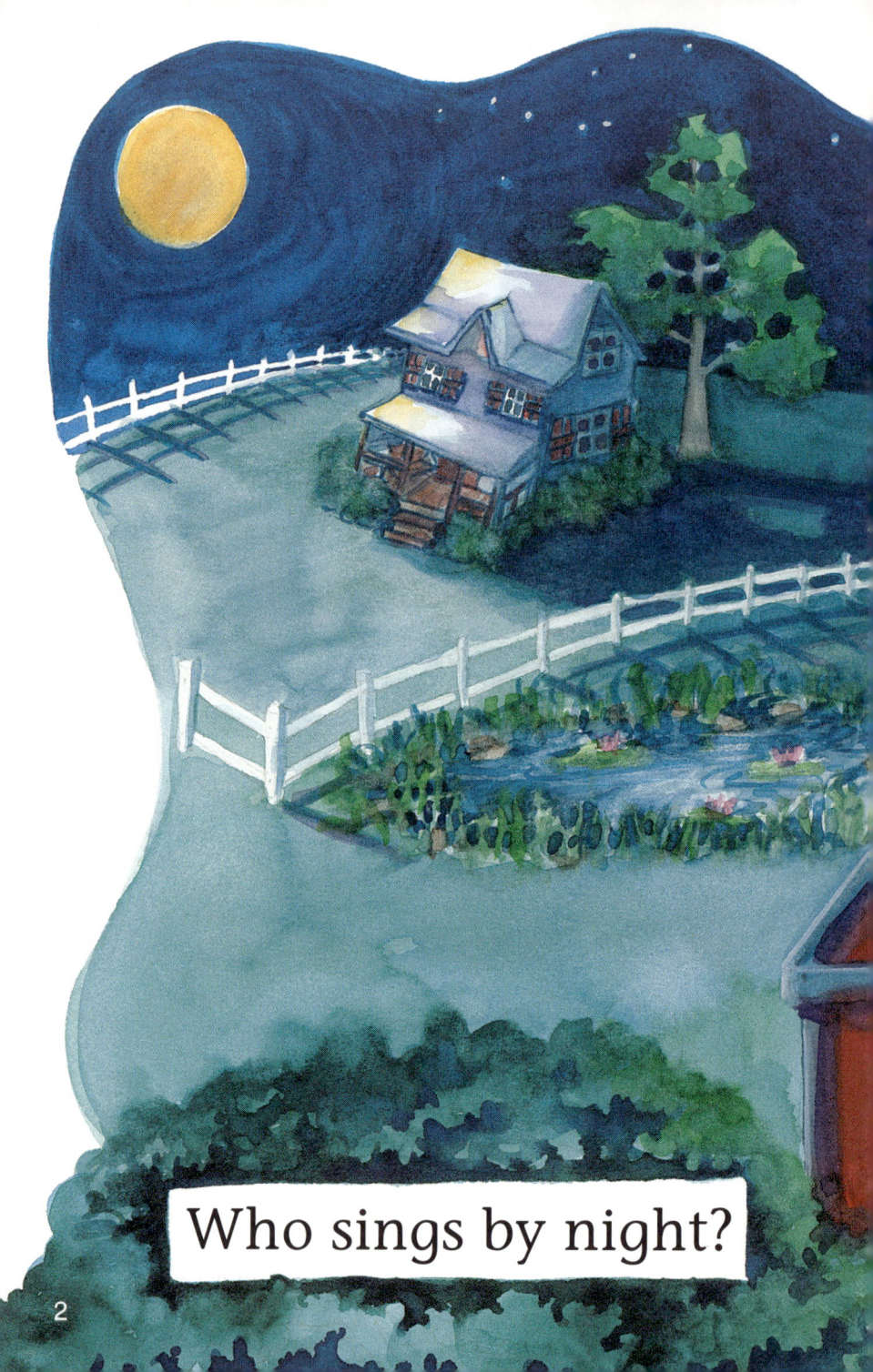

Who sings by night?

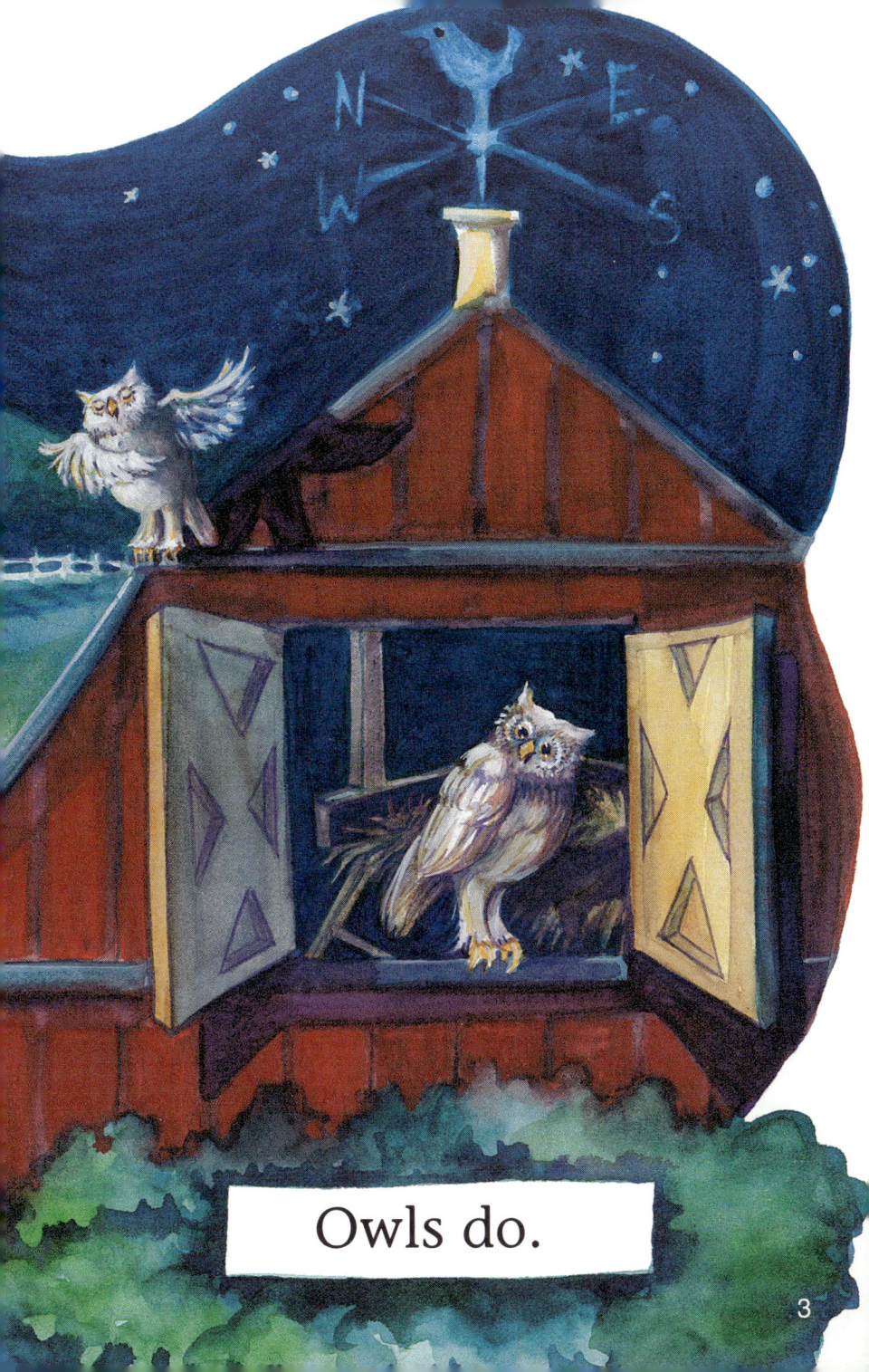

Owls do.

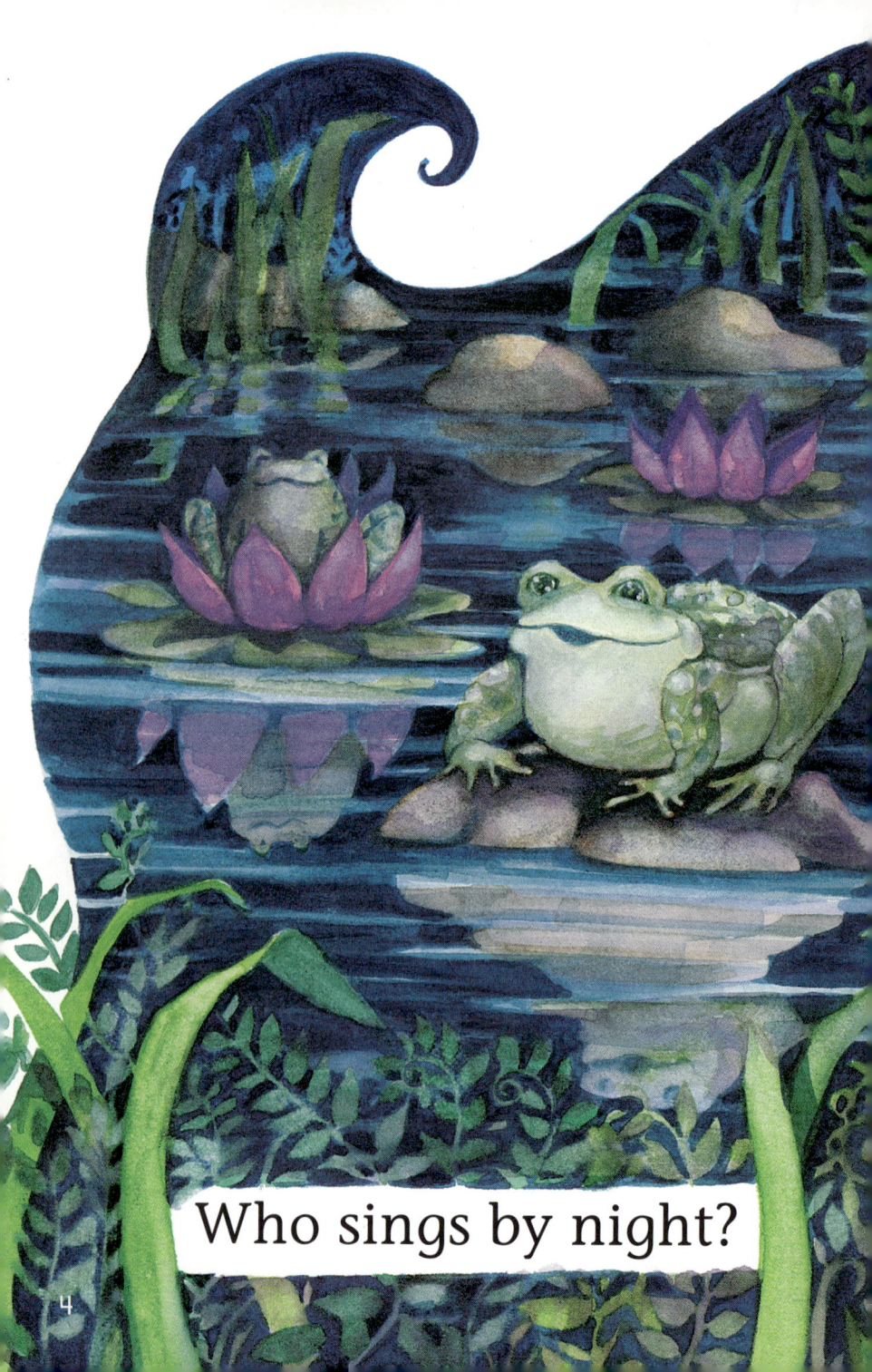

Who sings by night?

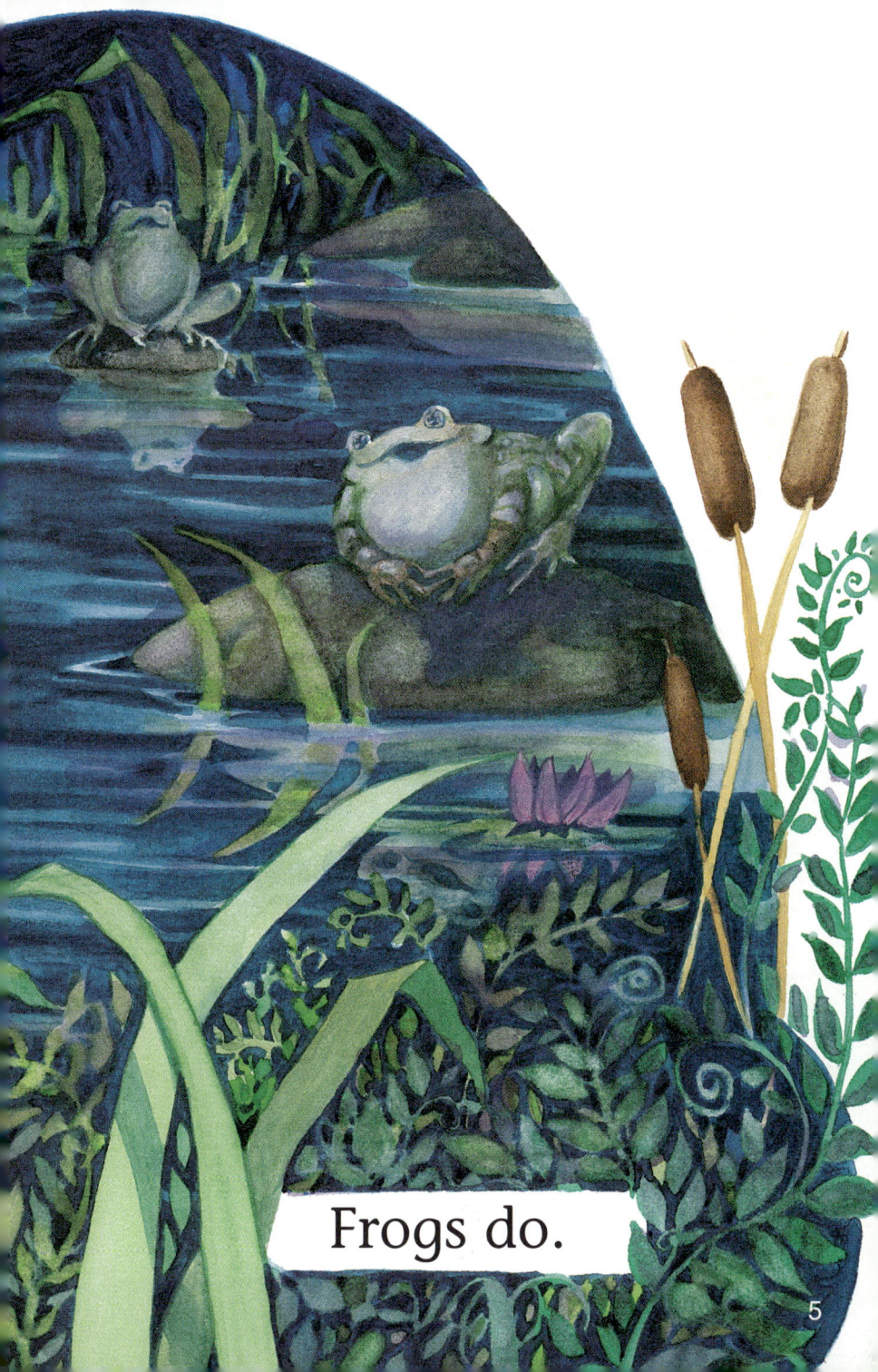

Frogs do.

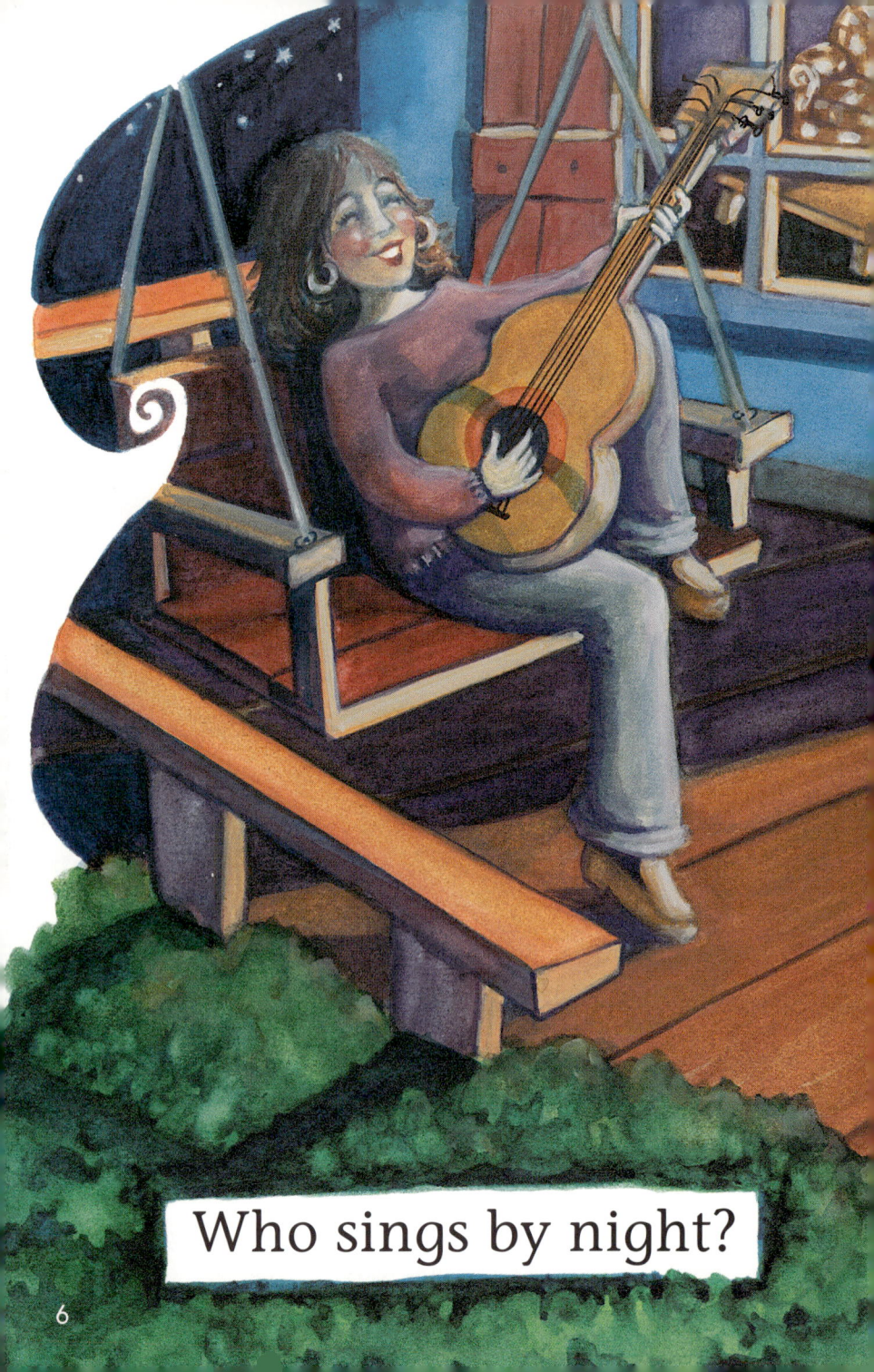

Who sings by night?

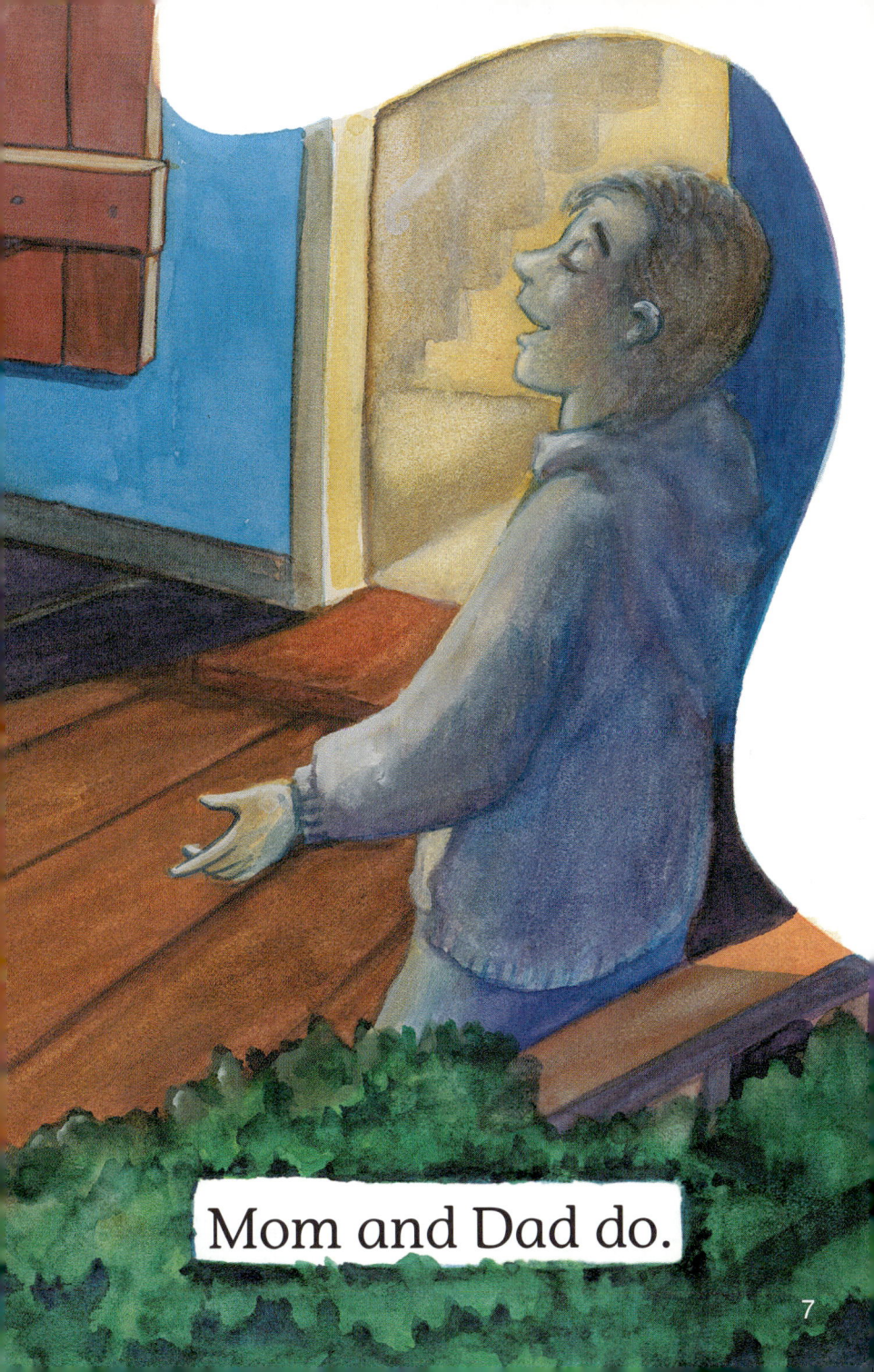

Mom and Dad do.

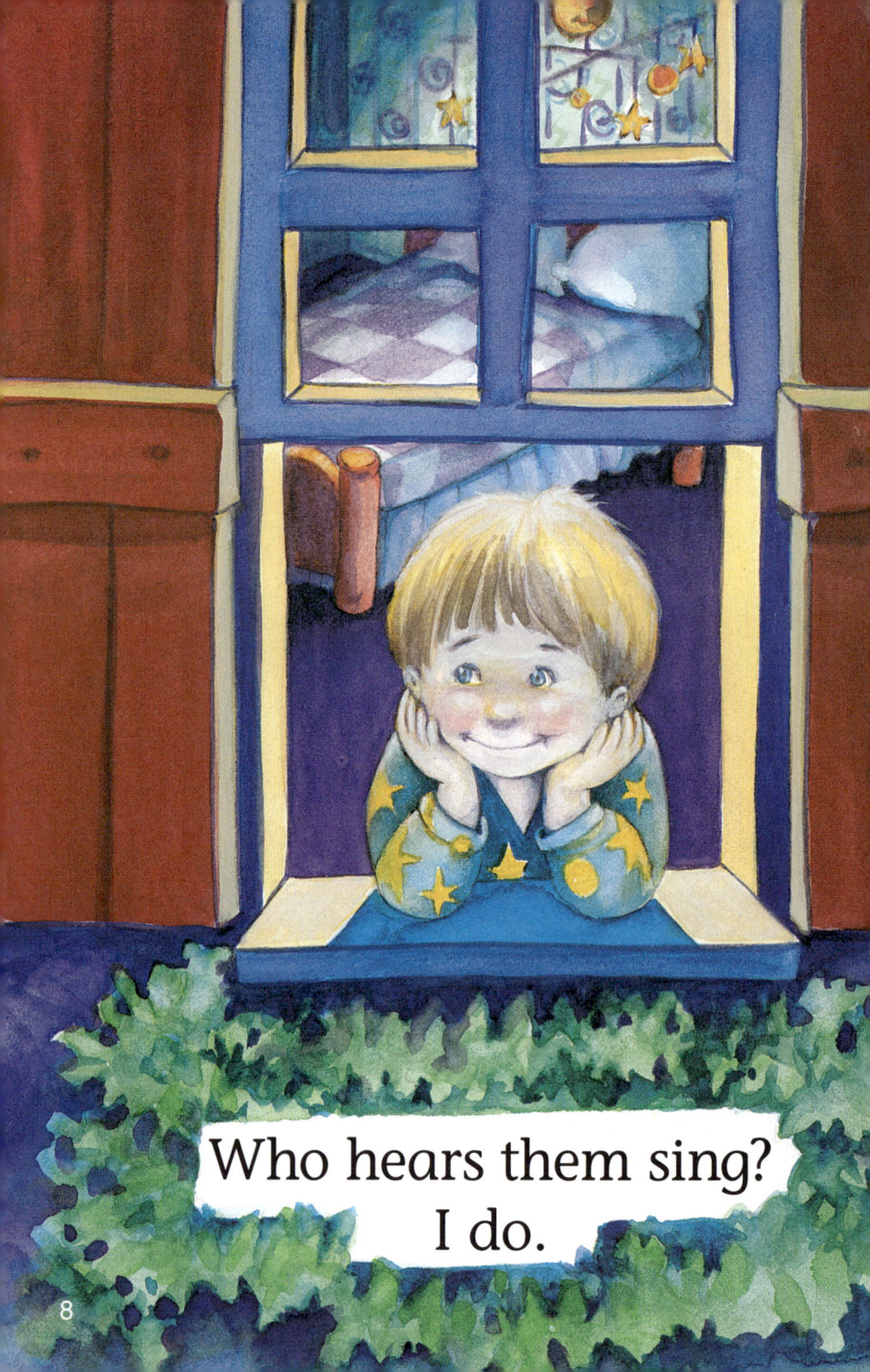

Who hears them sing?
I do.